501½ HORRIBLE FACTS

ARCTURUS

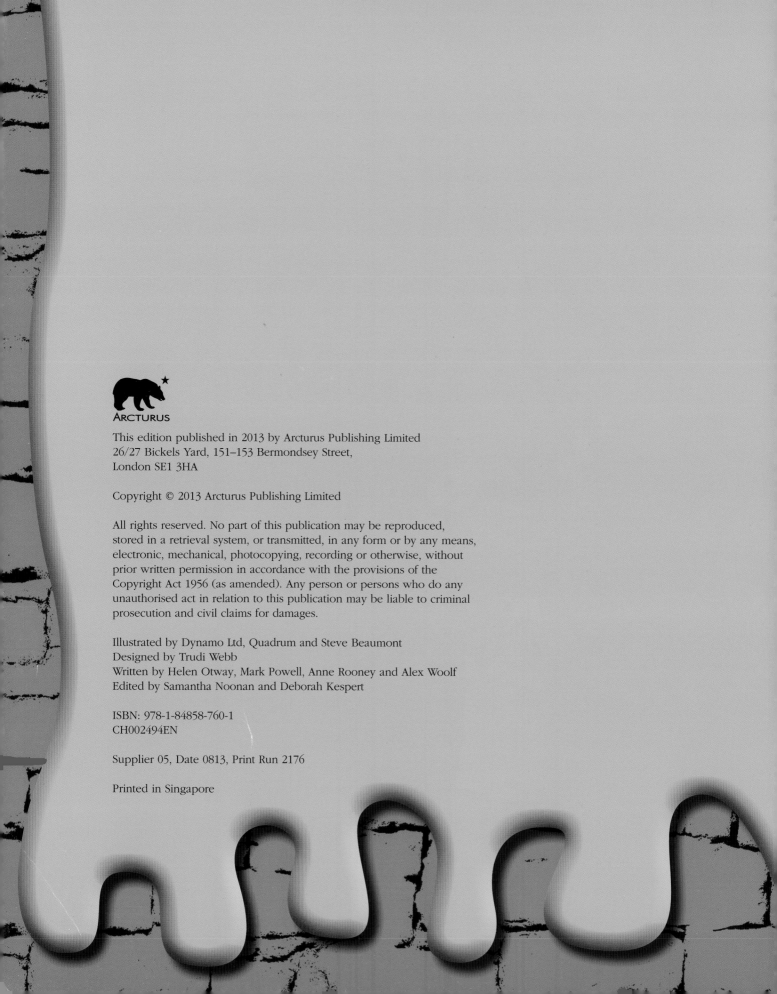

ARCTURUS

This edition published in 2013 by Arcturus Publishing Limited
26/27 Bickels Yard, 151–153 Bermondsey Street,
London SE1 3HA

Illustrated by Dynamo Ltd, Quadrum and Steve Beaumont
Designed by Trudi Webb
Written by Helen Otway, Mark Powell, Anne Rooney and Alex Woolf
Edited by Samantha Noonan and Deborah Kespert

ISBN: 978-1-84858-760-1
CH002494EN

Supplier 05, Date 0813, Print Run 2176

Printed in Singapore

CONTENTS

Horrible Body Facts 7

Horrible History Facts 35

Horrible Science Facts 65

Horrible Animal Facts 95

So you think you can **handle** this collection of the most **disgusting, yucky** and **downright dreadful** facts in the world?

Try these for starters....

- Whilst talking, you spit out 300 tiny drops of spit per minute!

- In medieval London, the combined excrement of humans and animals came to 50 tons a day.

- Houseflies poop roughly every four minutes.

- Butter and yoghurt made from camels' milk are green.

- The hairy frog of Central Africa breaks its own bones and pushes them through its skin as weapons!

It only gets worse from here, read on if you dare!

WARNING

THIS BOOK IS FILLED WITH THE STRANGE, THE GROSS AND THE DISTURBING.

No matter how interesting you find the facts and events recorded on these pages, please do not attempt to try any of them at home.

You will end up ill, maimed or worse!

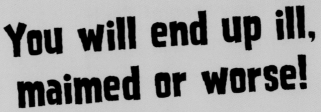

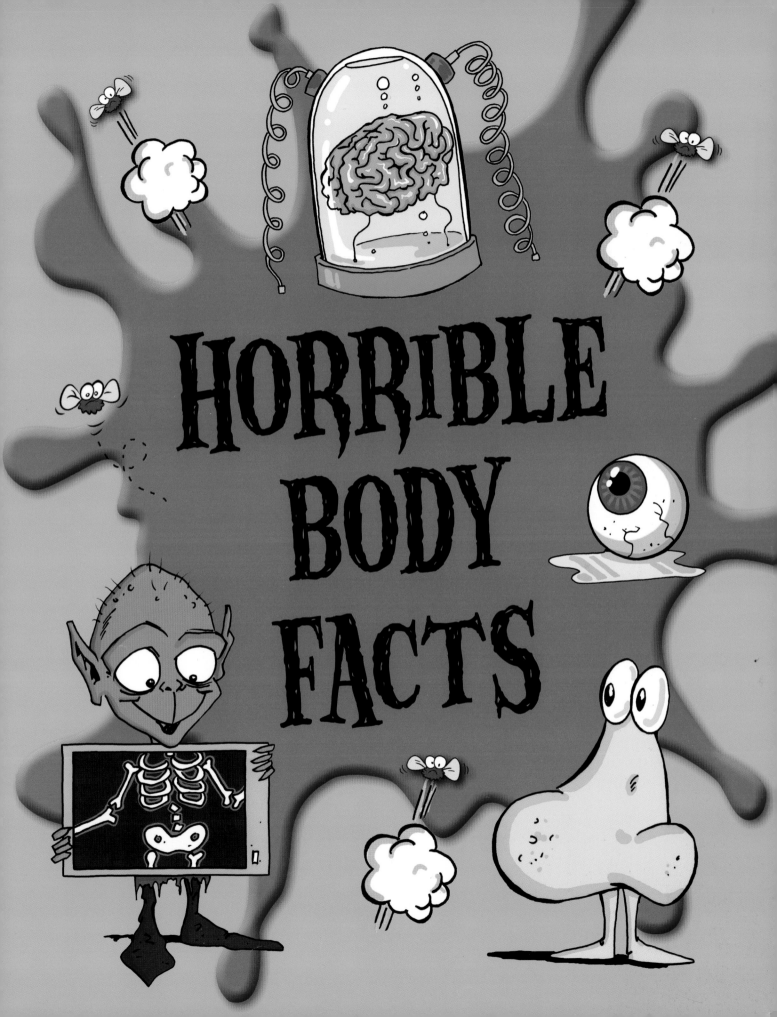

HORRIBLE BODY FACTS

BEASTLY BODY

Men have more nose hair than women... and it grows longer as they get older!

Sweat is made mainly of water, so it doesn't smell... until it's been around a while. Once skin bacteria have had time to slurp it up and multiply, the whiff begins.

Gross!

You have mucus in your eyes! It's there to make your tear fluid spread evenly.

There are millions of things living in your mouth! Don't bother looking though – they are microorganisms that are too small to see.

If you kept all your loose eyelashes and lined them up, they would stretch about 30 m (100 ft). Hopefully you'll find better ways to spend your retirement...

A carbuncle is a large abscess on the skin that oozes pus.

Nose-pickings are a mixture of dried mucus and what is filtered out of the air you breathe - pollen, dust, fungus, dirt, maybe the odd bug and even tiny particles of dust from space!

There is a fungal infection that causes the taste buds to swell and darken, giving the tongue a black, furry appearance.

The little pink lump in the corner of your eye is what remains of an extra eyelid that our ancestors had.

If your dead skin cells didn't drop off, after three years your skin would be as thick as an elephant's!

It takes just over 3 kg (7 lb) of pressure to tear off a human ear. Don't try it!

Your belly button is the scar left from your umbilical cord. Whether it's an 'innie' or an 'outie' depends on the shape and size of your umbilical cord when you were born.

0.2 % of the world's population has an extra finger or toe. That's 12 million people with an extra digit or two!

SQUIDGY BITS

Make your hand into a fist – that's how big your heart is!

One in 600 people are born with kidneys that are fused together in a horseshoe shape.

A teratoma is a rare growth that can have hair and teeth!

When it is empty, your bladder is all wrinkly.

You've got jelly in your bones! It is called bone marrow and it makes your blood cells.

If you could remove your brain and spread it out, it would be the size of a pillowcase.

The lungs can survive longer than any other organ after being removed from the body.

The body's largest internal organ is the liver. It's also one of the busiest. It has more than 500 jobs to do and needs two blood supplies.

Pig hearts are similar to ours, so pig heart valves are sometimes used in heart surgery to replace faulty human ones.

13

ALL ABOUT BLOOD

A single drop of blood contains 250 million blood cells.

Gross!

Mosquito saliva contains parasites which cause malaria. When they bite, the parasites travel through the victim's bloodstream and multiply in the liver and red blood cells.

Only a few hundred people in the world have the rarest blood type, which is H-H. They can't receive blood transfusions from any other blood group.

During a severe nosebleed, blood can travel up through the sinuses and come out of the eyes.

14

BONES AND MUSCLES

One person in 20 has an extra pair of ribs. If the extra bones cause problems, they can be removed.

Your bendiest muscles are the ones in your tongue!

A caterpillar has more muscles in its body than you do!

Some contortionists dislocate their hip or shoulder joints during their displays.

When you were born you had more than 300 bones, but you'll have only 206 by the time you finish growing! Don't worry, you won't lose them along the way – some of your smaller bones will just fuse together to make bigger bones.

Some of your body's muscles stretch to twice their relaxed length when you exercise.

You sit on the largest muscles in your body! You have a gluteus maximus in each buttock.

After French artist Henri de Toulouse-Lautrec broke his legs in his early teens, they stopped growing. As an adult, he had a fully grown torso and child-sized legs.

You have a tailbone at the end of your spine! It is called the coccyx, meaning 'cuckoo', because it looks like a cuckoo's beak.

17

HORRIBLE HAIR, TEETH AND NAILS

Nail fungus, bacteria and viruses lurk in nail files... so it's best not to share, just in case!

Cola is more acidic than vinegar... and acid destroys the enamel on your teeth, so remember to brush well!

They may look different, but your hair and fingernails are made from the same stuff: keratin. Cows' horns and lions' claws are made from it too!

Bill Black, a barber from the USA, made shirts, ties and even a bikini out of hair clippings!

It takes six hours for a coating of plaque to form after cleaning your teeth. If you don't brush it off, it eventually becomes tartar, a rock-hard substance that your dentist has to scrape off.

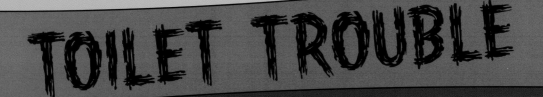

TOILET TROUBLE

The average person loses 200 ml (7 fl oz) of water a day in their poop.

Yuk!

Fancy a Japanese bird poop facial? The special enzymes in the droppings of the Japanese Bush Warbler make it an ingredient in some anti-wrinkle treatments.

Poop smells largely because the microbes in your gut produce two stinky chemicals as they work to break down your food – indole and skatole.

About a third of your poop is not old food, but bacteria that help you to digest food, and bits of the lining of the inside of your gut.

Coprophagy is the word used for eating poop!

The amount of toilet paper used in the USA in one day would go around the world nine times.

If you ever want to classify what you leave behind in the toilet, you should take a look at the Bristol Stool Chart. The seven types of stool listed range from 'separate hard lumps, like nuts' (Type 1) to 'entirely liquid' (Type 7).

SNOT, PUS & GUNK

A bad gum infection called gingivitis can lead to pus-filled mouth sores, purple gums and the stinkiest of stinky breath.

Your nose is busy making mucus all day long, but you swallow most of it - about one cupful. Gross!

Rotten teeth can lead to gum boils. If one of these bursts, your mouth is filled with pus!

People in ancient India inoculated themselves against smallpox by rubbing pus from an infected person into a scratch on their bodies.

Earwax tastes very bitter. If you must try it, make sure no one's looking...

Pus is a gooey yellow cocktail of dead cells, bacteria, proteins and white blood cells.

Nose mucus is normally clear and runny, but if you have a bacterial infection it will turn thick and yellow, or even green!

One treatment for pus-filled abscesses is to cut in to the skin and scoop out all the pus!

If your vomit looks like what you've just eaten, that's exactly what it is. If it's soupy, then it's because it's been in your stomach for a while.

If you throw up and your vomit is greenish, it contains bile from your intestine, not just your stomach. Bile and stomach acid make vomit taste awful.

The biggest recorded distance for projectile vomiting is 8 m (27 ft)!

Vomiting a lot can give you a black eye! The pressure causes blood vessels to burst.

Vomit is a yucky cocktail of half-digested food, stomach mucus, saliva and gastric acids.

24

NASTY NOISES & STINKY SMELLS

French doctor Frédéric Saldmann insists that people should burp, fart and sweat freely to reduce the risk of cancer.

Gross!

The average man produces enough gas per day to blow up a small balloon!

The 250,000 sweat glands in your feet make them one of the sweatiest parts of the body. Adults produce two whole cups of that stinky foot juice every week!

Does your tummy ever rumble or growl? The proper name for it is 'borborygmus' and it's the sound of muscles contracting in your digestive system.

When a dead body is decomposing, the bacteria inside it produce gases. When the gas is released from the body, it sounds like a fart!

The air you force out when you cough can reach speeds of 60 miles (100 km) an hour.

If you eat asparagus, your urine will smell of rotten cabbages! The whiff comes from a gas called methanethiol, which is produced when you digest the vegetable.

Yuk!

What you hear when you fart is the vibration of your sphincter muscles as air passes through them. The sort of sound you get depends on how fast the air is going.

GHASTLY DISEASES

There are more than 2,500 types of mosquito worldwide, spreading viruses and parasites that kill millions of people every year.

Emetophobia is a fear of vomiting.

Black flies breed in fast-flowing rivers and spread a worm that destroys human eyes. This tropical disease is called river blindness.

Rat fleas spread the deadly disease bubonic plague. Although it's rare these days, the illness killed around one-third of the population of 14th-century Europe, when it was known as 'The Black Death.'

One of the most common waterborne diseases worldwide is cryptosporidiosis. Microscopic parasites, swallowed in infected water, hatch inside the intestine and cause uncontrollable pooping.

Weil's disease is a serious infection that causes jaundice and kidney damage. It comes from rats' urine and is usually caught from drinking infected water.

Sand flies spread the parasitic disease leishmaniasis through their bites. The parasites cause boils on the skin, which can last for up to a year and leave bad scars. If they find their way into the body, the parasites can also damage the internal organs.

Malaria kills more than one million people every year.

WORMS & WORSE!

You don't have to ingest hookworms to catch them – they can bore through the skin on your feet!

You have at least a million dust mites crawling around your mattress and pillow, gobbling up all your old skin cells.

In a severe case of worms, a large group can clump together in a ball and cause a blockage in the intestines.

The female chigoe flea lays her eggs by burrowing into human skin head first, leaving her back end sticking out. Over two weeks, she feeds on blood and lays about 100 eggs, before dying and falling out.

30

Demodex mites are tiny parasites that live in eyebrows and eyelashes. They're very common, especially in older people. Under a microscope, they look like worms with stubby legs.

The average human body is host to over a million parasites.

The best reason to check for head lice is the saying 'what goes in must come out'. Yep, if they're feeding on your blood, they're pooping in your hair!

A tapeworm can grow in the intestine for decades, reaching a length of 10 m (33 ft). Worst of all, you may not even know you have one...

MONSTROUS MEDICINE

Robert Liston was the fastest surgeon in 19th-century Scotland. He could carry out an amputation in just 30 seconds.

Gross!

One medieval treatment for a skin infection was to rub cow dung on it.

Early X-rays caused nasty side effects such as skin burns, swelling and hair loss.

Foreign bodies can occasionally get left behind during operations. Things that have been sewn inside patients include clamps, surgical sponges, scalpels, scissors, forceps and doctors. Okay, only kidding about the last one!

Ancient Romans used to clean their teeth with urine. Mmm, refreshing!

Pliny the Elder, an ancient Roman, said eating lion fat was a cure for epilepsy. If there were no lions around, sufferers could always try one of his other suggestions – dried camel's brain in vinegar!

Hippocrates, who is sometimes called the founder of modern medicine, believed that coughs could be cured by violently shaking the sufferer up and down.

Yuk!

A 16th-century treatment for baldness was to clean the head with a shampoo made from crushed beetles, then rub a nice bit of fox fat on it.

DID YOU KNOW?

- If you swim for an hour in a public pool, you will swallow about 80 ml (2.7 fl oz) of urine.

- Most body gas comes from swallowed air, and the rest from fermentation of undigested food.

- You can buy mini vacuum cleaners for your ears!

- Fresh urine is cleaner than spit or the skin on your face because it does not contain bacteria.

- Maoni Vi from Cape Town, South Africa, has armpit hair that is 81 cm (32 in) long!

- Women of the Himalayan Apatani tribe used to enlarge their nostrils with circular 25 mm (1 in) wide noseplugs.

- When you pee, a small amount of urine enters your mouth through your saliva.

- Some Eskimo mothers suck snot out of their babies' noses with their mouths.

- A US company has started making underwear that captures and masks the smell of farts!

- The deadliest natural toxin, clostridium botulinum, comes from bad food.

- British performer Scott Bell has walked 100 m (328 ft) over burning hot embers.

- Sometimes, waste products clump in the kidneys to create very painful kidney stones!

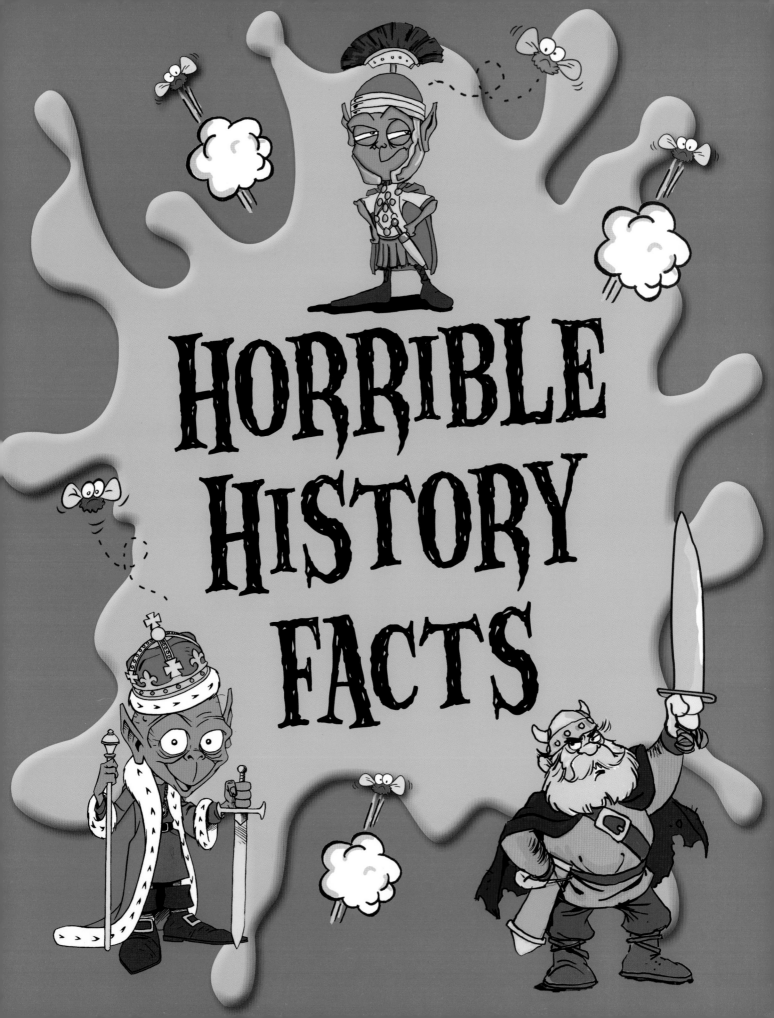

HORRIBLE HISTORY FACTS

HIDEOUS HISTORY

The Romans had criminals torn apart by wild animals while the public watched. Animals were brought from all over the Roman Empire, but dogs and lions were the most popular.

Romans who killed a relative would be executed by being tied in a sack with a live dog, a rooster, a snake and a monkey and thrown into a river.

In ancient Rome, urine was collected from public toilets and used as a clothes dye, a hair product and an ingredient in toothpaste.

People with warts in the Middle Ages would pay a wart charmer to get rid of them.

The Incas of South America used to mummify their dead kings and leave them sitting on their thrones.

Some ancient African tribes used animal dung to stiffen their hair. No point in washing it first then!

Following his execution in 1618, Sir Walter Raleigh's wife kept his embalmed head in a red leather bag for 29 years. She even carried it around with her until it got too smelly...

Early candles were made from cow fat or whale blubber.

In ancient Egypt, women kept a cone of grease on their heads. During the day, it melted in the hot sun and dripped down, making their hair gleam with grease.

AWFUL ANCIENT TIMES

In Jericho around 7,000 years ago, people buried their dead under the dirt floors of their houses.

Gross!

Remains found in a mass grave in South Dakota, USA, show that prehistoric warriors scalped their victims, probably to keep the hair as a trophy.

The ancient Aztecs used to sacrifice humans by cutting out their hearts!

When men of the Iron Age died, their horses would often be killed and buried with them.

14,000 years ago, people in Florida, USA, would impale turtles on sticks and roast them over a fire to eat.

PUTRID PYRAMIDS

Pharaoh Pepy II of Egypt always kept several naked slaves with him whose bodies were smeared with honey. This encouraged flies to land on them instead of him! A very sticky business...

Gross!

Before embalming the body, a pharaoh's vital organs (the lungs, liver, stomach and intestines) were removed and stored in special jars in the tomb.

Careless embalmers accidentally wrapped flies, lizards and even a mouse into some mummies' bandages!

When Pharaoh Ramesses II was mummified in 1212 BC, the embalmers tried to keep his nose in shape by stuffing it with peppercorns!

Ancient Egyptians used a special long-handled spoon to scoop out a corpse's brain – through the nose – before mummification.

Yuk!

Ancient Egyptians treated some infections with spoiled bread. As it happens, rotting bread contains antibiotics, so it probably worked.

Pharaoh Hatshepsut wore a false, braided beard as part of her royal outfit.

41

GRUESOME GREEKS

Ancient Greeks didn't use napkins. Instead, they wiped their hands on pieces of bread, then fed the bread to dogs.

Ancient Greek philosopher Heraclitus tried to cure swelling in his legs by burying himself in animal dung!

A sumptuous feast in ancient Greece might include any of these yummy morsels: sea urchins, thrushes, peacock eggs, grasshoppers or a pig that had died from eating too much.

Both the Greeks and Romans believed they could tell the future by examining the pattern made by the guts spilled from a sacrificed bird. The future always looked grim for birds...

Many ancient Greek Olympic events were carried out naked. Hmm...!

Greek doctors were first permitted to dissect bodies over 2,000 years ago. They were also allowed to perform vivisection (the cutting up of live bodies) on criminals.

The ancient Greek death penalty was to drink a poison called hemlock.

A Greek cure for bad breath was to boil the head of a hare together with three mice and rub the resulting mixture on your gums. It probably covered up the original smell, but wasn't necessarily any better!

43

REVOLTING ROMANS

Ancient Roman whips were especially vicious – they had pieces of bone or metal on the end.

The Roman Emperor Nero tied Christians to poles, covered them in pitch and burnt them at his parties!

To clean themselves, Romans poured olive oil all over their bodies then scraped off the oily, dirty gunk with a curved blade called a strigil. Yuk!

People living in the ancient town of Pompeii were trapped under deep volcanic ash when Mount Vesuvius erupted in AD79. When the bodies decomposed, they left their shapes behind in the ash. Plaster casts have been made so visitors today can see recreations of the people who died.

Ancient Roman physician Galen was a pioneer of cataract surgery, using long needles on sufferers' eyes. This was in the days before anesthetics!

Under the Roman king Tarquinius Priscus, people who committed suicide were crucified... even though they were already dead!

Ancient Romans spread pigeon droppings on their hair to lighten it – the ammonia acted as a bleach. You wouldn't have wanted to work in a hairdresser's in those days...

Roman gladiators had to fight to the bitter end – any who stopped would be prodded with hot pokers to spur them on again.

45

MONSTROUS MIDDLE AGES

In the 12th century, people strapped the leg bones of sheep or pigs to their feet to use as ice skates. Let's hope they cleaned them first!

Anglo-Saxon peasants sometimes wore clothes made out of dried stinging nettles.

Medieval soldiers used to catapult things over castle walls at their enemies, including severed heads!

In the past, butchers would kill animals for meat inside their stores, then throw the innards out into the street.

46

In the Middle Ages a
royal farter was employed
to jump around farting in
front of the king
to amuse him.

People in the
Middle Ages
made washing
powder from
wood ash
and urine.

So many people died from
the Black Death that the corpses
had to be thrown into huge plague pits
that could hold hundreds
of bodies.

In Anglo-Saxon England,
people who died in a famine
were sometimes eaten by other
people who lived nearby!

The plague of Justinian spread
all over Europe between AD541 and 542. At its
worst it killed between 5,000 and 10,000 people
every day. Often, there wasn't enough room to
bury the dead, so bodies were left
rotting in the streets.

47

MAD MODERN TIMES

During World War II, the Soviet army used dogs strapped with explosives to blow up German tanks.

After the death of Lenin in 1924, his brain was entrusted to a respected doctor who (it was hoped) would be able to revive the Soviet leader...

During the civil war of 1989-1996 in Liberia, Africa, General Joshua Milton Blahyi was famous for leading his army into battle naked - except for his boots and gun. His nickname was 'General Butt-Naked'!

Up until 1935, manufacturing methods meant that toilet paper sometimes had splinters in it. Ouch!

The first animal in space was a dog called Laika, who was sent into orbit in the Soviet satellite Sputnik 2 in 1957. Laika died of stress and overheating, but she will be remembered in the history books forever!

German scientist Fritz Haber was given a Nobel prize for his work on fertilizers. He is also known as the father of chemical warfare due to his work on poisonous gases in World War I.

The world's biggest food fight occurs every year on the last Wednesday of August. Since 1944, the town of Bunol in Spain has hosted an annual festival called La Tomatina in which 40,000 people pelt each other with tomatoes!

49

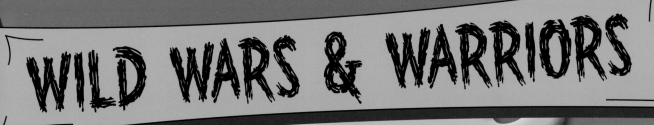

WILD WARS & WARRIORS

New Scythian soldiers had to drink the blood of the first enemy soldier they killed.

When the British warrior-queen Boudicca marched on the Roman town of Londinium (London) her army killed 70,000 people.

The enemies of Roman Emperor Valerian killed him by pouring molten gold down his throat.

Many medieval knights died because of their protective metal suits. Some of them baked to death when they were fighting in hot countries!

When the first emperor of China died in 210 BC, an army of 7,500 clay soldiers was placed around his tomb at Mount Li. The tomb was also booby-trapped, so that anyone who tried to break in would be shot with an arrow.

If they were feeling really bloodthirsty, Vikings killed their enemies using the 'blood eagle' - they cut and opened out the victim's ribs like the wings of an eagle, then removed the lungs.

Yuk!

The terrifying 15th-century warrior Pier Gerlofs Donia was known for his ability to chop off several enemies' heads with one swing of his great sword.

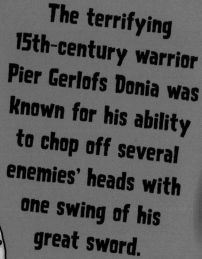

DEATH & DISEASE

One symptom of smallpox was black pox – the skin took on a charred appearance, turning black and peeling off.

Charles VI of France suffered from a mental illness that made him believe his body was made of glass.

Pope Clement VII tried eating a death cap toadstool in 1534, which killed him.

In the 1800s, there were several cases of people being buried when not really dead. There were terrible stories about opened coffins with scratch marks on the inside, and corpses with fingernails worn away by trying to escape.

In the 19th century, London had a train service for the dead! Mourners and coffin bearers would depart from Necropolis Station and get off at Cemetery Station, where the funerals were held in Brookwood Cemetery.

Victims of the 1918 flu pandemic had such bad lung damage that their faces turned blue or purple and they coughed up blood.

A terrible plague killed a third of the population of Athens in 430BC. Victims had a fever, headaches, stomach pain, vomiting and were covered in painful blisters. Those that didn't die often lost fingers, toes or their sight. Historians still don't know what the disease was.

In times of famine, Stone Age tribes would eat old women before dogs because they were considered less useful!

53

TERRIBLE TREATMENTS

Ancient Egyptian doctors used acacia thorns as needles when they stitched up wounds.

A popular Victorian beauty treatment contained arsenic, vinegar and chalk. What's a little arsenic poisoning if you have perfect skin?

An early typhus vaccine was made from squished body lice that were infected with the deadly disease!

Ancient Roman, Pliny the Elder advised people with toothache to cure themselves by catching a frog under a full moon and spitting into its mouth!

Eighteenth-century toothpaste recipes included burnt bread and dragon's blood. It's not quite as gruesome as it sounds – dragon's blood was a red plant resin.

Some surgeons in ancient times tried using pig skin for nose reconstructions on people. When the skin dried up and dropped off, they believed it was because the pig had died!

Tudors used to cure headaches by rubbing their foreheads with the rope used to hang a criminal!

Blood-sucking leeches were first used as a medical treatment by the ancient Egyptians.

55

SLAUGHTER & TORTURE

Gross!

A Chinese torture chair from the 19th century has blades sticking up from the armrests and seat, and sticking out from the back. Ouch!

The 15th-century German king Wenceslas was so angry with his chef after a bad meal, that he had him roasted alive!

Samurai swords were rated for sharpness by how many (dead) human bodies they could slice through in one go. The best swords scored a rating of five bodies.

The Celts, who lived in Britain around 500BC, collected the heads of people they slaughtered in battle. They stuck them on poles, chucked them in rivers as gifts to the gods, nailed them to the walls as decorations or hollowed them out to use as cups.

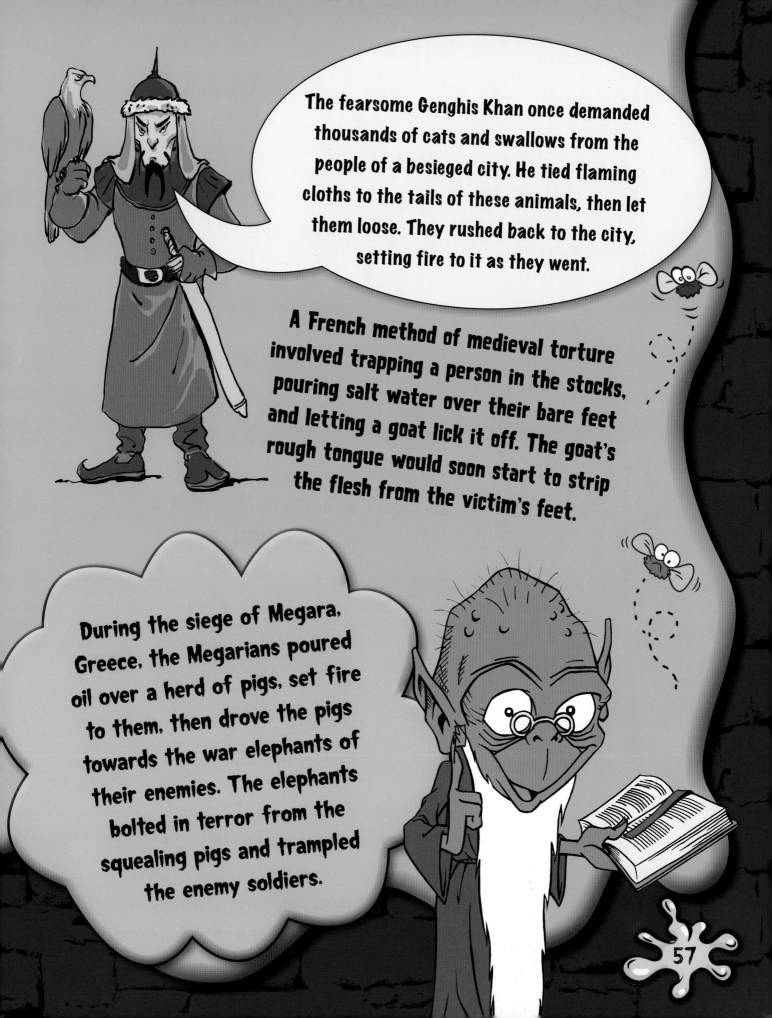

The fearsome Genghis Khan once demanded thousands of cats and swallows from the people of a besieged city. He tied flaming cloths to the tails of these animals, then let them loose. They rushed back to the city, setting fire to it as they went.

A French method of medieval torture involved trapping a person in the stocks, pouring salt water over their bare feet and letting a goat lick it off. The goat's rough tongue would soon start to strip the flesh from the victim's feet.

During the siege of Megara, Greece, the Megarians poured oil over a herd of pigs, set fire to them, then drove the pigs towards the war elephants of their enemies. The elephants bolted in terror from the squealing pigs and trampled the enemy soldiers.

CRIME & PUNISHMENT

In 1750BC, the Babylonian king Hammurabi decided on a new set of punishments for criminals. These included cutting off a finger or hand for theft and cutting off a man's lower lip for kissing a married woman.

Public hangings were stopped in England in 1868. They were so crowded that too many people were hurt or killed in the crush to see the action!

In Victorian times, Mary Ann Cotton poisoned three husbands and fifteen of her children!

Chicago gangster Dion O'Banion was given a lavish funeral in 1924, with 10,000 mourners paying their respects. The biggest and most expensive wreath came from Al Capone, the gangster who had ordered O'Banion's murder!

The 17th-century Italian lady's poison of choice was Acqua Toffana: a lethal cocktail of arsenic, lead and belladonna (deadly nightshade). Perfect for using on an annoying husband!

A medieval punishment for murderers was to have each arm and leg tied to a different horse, then the four horses were made to run in different directions, tearing the criminal apart.

In 1924, the state of Nevada, USA, decided that hanging and shooting were too barbaric as a means of execution. So they introduced the gas chamber instead.

The most common punishments in the Middle Ages were death, exile and mutilation - lovely!

FOUL FAMOUS PEOPLE

Mongol leader Tamerlane played polo with the skulls of people he had killed in battle.

When Ivan the Terrible found out his sixth wife was having an affair, he had her boyfriend impaled on a spike and left to die outside her bedroom window.

It is said that Attila the Hun (who ruled the Hun kingdom between 434–453) enjoyed the taste of raw flesh and human blood. Saved on cooking...

On October 25th 1760, King George II became the second English king to die on the toilet.

60

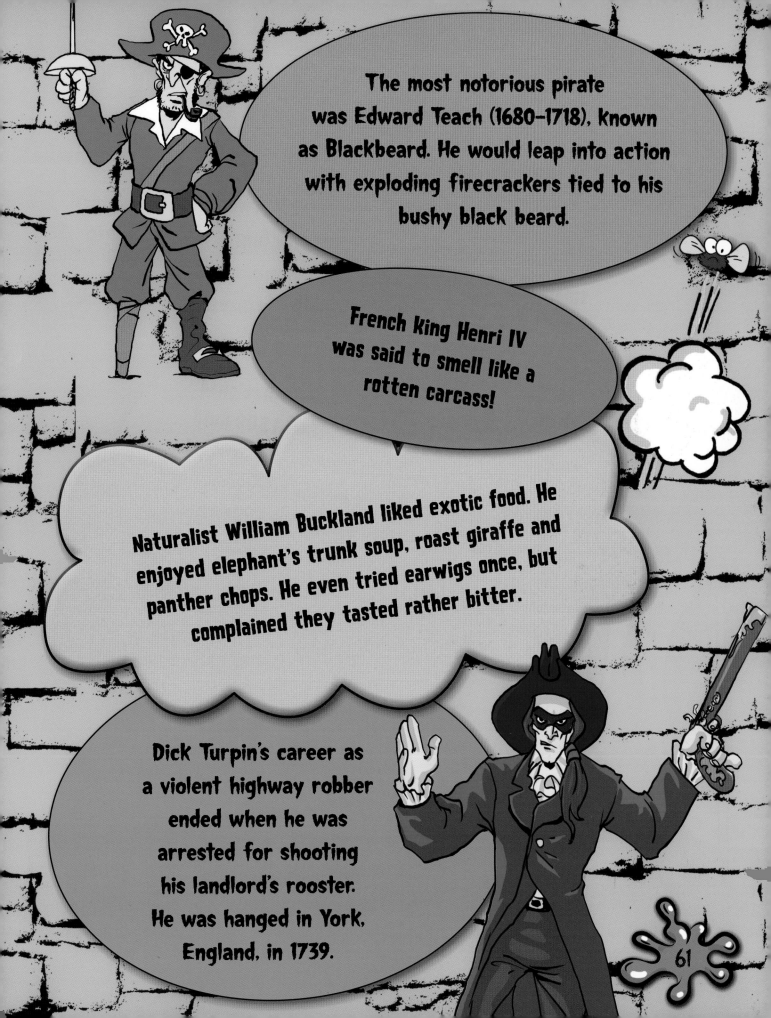

The most notorious pirate was Edward Teach (1680–1718), known as Blackbeard. He would leap into action with exploding firecrackers tied to his bushy black beard.

French king Henri IV was said to smell like a rotten carcass!

Naturalist William Buckland liked exotic food. He enjoyed elephant's trunk soup, roast giraffe and panther chops. He even tried earwigs once, but complained they tasted rather bitter.

Dick Turpin's career as a violent highway robber ended when he was arrested for shooting his landlord's rooster. He was hanged in York, England, in 1739.

REPULSIVE ROYALTY

King Francis I of France, who ruled between 1515 and 1547, always carried with him a small piece of an ancient Egyptian mummy! He used it as a medicine to soothe bruises.

Gross!

Tudor King Henry VIII reigned over England from 1509 until his death in 1547, and married six times. The lucky ones escaped with divorce - two had their heads chopped off!

Queen Victoria of England survived eight assassination attempts!

After William the Conqueror's death in 1087, his body swelled up with gas as he started to decompose. On the day of his funeral, his stomach exploded, causing a terrible stench!

Queen Elizabeth I of England had very bad teeth, but was so afraid of having one taken out that a loyal archbishop had to have one of his teeth removed first to reassure her.

Henry VIII's second wife, Anne Boleyn was believed to have had eleven fingers.

Hung Wu, the first emperor of the Ming dynasty in China, was so fearful of the rebellious city of Peiping, that in 1368 he ordered the entire city to be destroyed.

Yuk!

Fierce Catholic Mary I of England, known as 'Bloody Mary', executed more than 200 Protestants when she reigned over England between 1553 and 1558.

DID YOU KNOW?

- In rural Germany, people put piles of poop in their front yards to show how wealthy they were.

- Only half of children born in Elizabethan times would live past their fifth birthday.

- The ancient Egyptians thought the brain was the least important organ, so they threw it away when they were making a mummy!

- In the 19th century, baking soda contained bone ash.

- In Anglo-Saxon times, shepherds were given twelve days' worth of manure at Christmas.

- Vikings used rancid butter to style and dress their hair.

- Early colonists in America used to clean their windows with rags dipped in urine.

- In China, in the 16th century, a common method of committing suicide was by eating a pound of salt.

- Scottish bagpipes were originally made from the stomach of a dead sheep.

- In Europe, over 100,000 people have been tried for witchcraft since 1100.

- People used to believe that smearing their clothes with fat from a dead pig would keep away the fleas.

- Some women used to drink turpentine in the belief it would make their urine smell like roses.

HORRIBLE SCIENCE FACTS

FOUL FOOD SCIENCE

Your body cannot digest tomato seeds – they pass straight through your intestines. Eat some today and see for yourself!

Some packaged salads contain a chemical that is also found in poisonous antifreeze!

Although your gastric juices contain powerful acids, they cannot digest chewing gum. Small amounts will get through the digestive system, but too much can cause a serious blockage... so always spit it out.

Some Japanese monks tried to ensure their bodies would be preserved after death by eating a special diet of tree bark, roots and poisonous tea, made from tree sap.

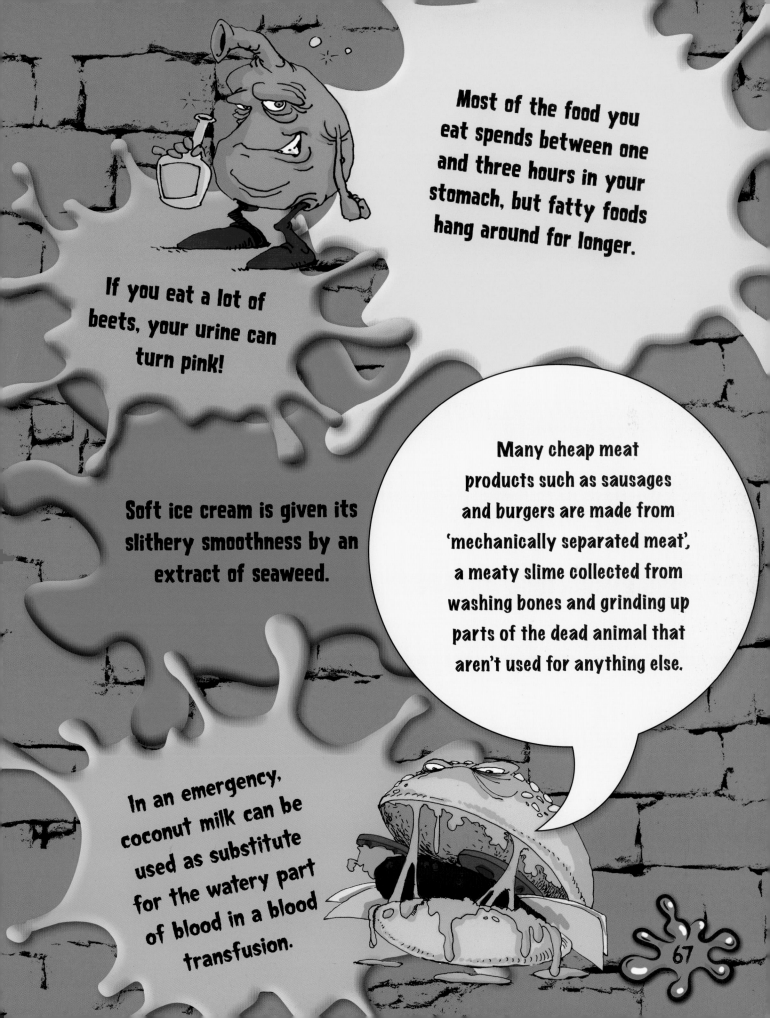

Most of the food you eat spends between one and three hours in your stomach, but fatty foods hang around for longer.

If you eat a lot of beets, your urine can turn pink!

Many cheap meat products such as sausages and burgers are made from 'mechanically separated meat', a meaty slime collected from washing bones and grinding up parts of the dead animal that aren't used for anything else.

Soft ice cream is given its slithery smoothness by an extract of seaweed.

In an emergency, coconut milk can be used as substitute for the watery part of blood in a blood transfusion.

SICK SCIENCE

You're more likely to get ill from kissing another person than a dog. Even though a dog's mouth has as many germs as a human's, not as many of them are harmful to us.

Our nearest galaxy, Andromeda, is heading for a collision with the Milky Way in the distant future. If Earth is near the collision site, it will disappear in less than a second!

The Japanese beetle, now common in the USA, can chew through a human eardrum.

Camel urine is thick and syrupy.

Scientists have recreated the deadly flu virus that killed 1% of the entire world population between 1918 and 1919. Smart, huh?

More than a billion people have a hookworm infection, which means they have tiny blood-sucking worms living in their intestine. All those hookworms suck a total of 10 million L (22 million pints) of blood a day!

Shaving a pregnant mouse makes her produce more milk and grow larger babies. A bald mouse can digest more food without overheating, and so makes more milk.

The bacteria E. coli was found on 10 % of coffee mugs in the USA.

A frog being sick was first observed when one was taken on a space flight.

69

PECULIAR PLANTS

Gross!

Stinging nettles grow well in soil that contains dead bodies – they thrive on a chemical called phosphorus which is in bones.

Scientists have created rice that contains human genes! Freaky...

The most poisonous plant in the world is the castor bean. Just 70 micrograms (2 millionths of an ounce) is enough to kill an adult human. It's 12,000 times more poisonous than rattlesnake venom.

The corpse flower or stinking lily is the smelliest flower in the world. Its stench is disgusting – it smells like a rotting corpse. This attracts insects that feed on dead matter, and they pollinate the flower.

A type of carnivorous plant found in the tropical rainforests of Asia can 'eat' birds and even rats. Animals are attracted by the nectar of the flower, and then fall into a vat of chemicals which dissolve them, feeding the plant.

Yuk!

The Australian bloodwood tree oozes red sap that looks like blood when it is cut.

Some trees communicate using chemicals. If a wood-eating bug attacks one, the tree releases chemicals into the air, prompting other trees in the area to produce a poison that deters the bugs.

LIVING EARTH

The largest living thing on Earth is a giant fungus that covers 4 square miles (10 sq km) in Oregon, USA. It is thought to be around 2,400 years old, but may be as old as 8,650 years!

Although humans need oxygen to survive, air that contains more than 50 % oxygen is toxic to us!

The anacampseros plant looks like a bird poop to protect it from being eaten by animals.

An African mushroom, called the Lady in the Veil, grows faster than any other organism in the world. It grows up to 20 cm (8 in) in only 20 minutes, and can be heard cracking as it grows!

In recent years, a poisonous spider called the false widow has colonized southern England. It arrived in bunches of bananas, and warm weather has allowed it to survive. There are now tens of thousands running wild!

Parts of the Atacama Desert in Chile have had no rain for 400 years.

Some types of plants and animals have evolved to live in the most hostile places; such as inside volcanic vents, at the bottom of vast caves, and even in the baking desert.

Fossilized cockroaches have been found to be 300 million years old. This means they existed 100 million years before the dinosaurs!

73

WACKY EXPERIMENTS

In 1804, trainee doctor Stubbins Firth tried to prove that yellow fever is not an infectious disease by drinking his patients' vomit! Although he did not get yellow fever, he was wrong. It is very contagious, but must enter directly through the bloodstream.

In 2002, Gunther von Hagens carried out a public autopsy in London, England. It was the first one for 170 years and was illegal. The police attended but did not arrest von Hagens. It was even on television!

Early polio vaccines contained ground-up monkey spinal cords and monkey kidney tissues.

Phosphorous (the chemical used for making matches) was first created when chemists extracted it from their urine.

The slime produced by a slug creates a small electric current when smeared over copper. Slug-powered phone anyone?

A Swiss journalist named Etienne Dumont is growing horns on his head. He has silicon implants under the skin and as the skin grows over them he replaces them with slightly larger ones.

American inventor, Thomas Edison, electrocuted several animals, including a zoo elephant, in his research on electricity.

18th-century Italian scientist Lazzaro Spallanzani often made himself throw up to get samples of stomach acid for his experiments.

75

NATURAL DISASTERS

The lava (molten rock) that erupts out of a volcano can be as hot as 1,200 degrees Celsius (2,200 degrees Fahrenheit) and the power of a large eruption can equal that of several hundred nuclear bombs.

Aaah!

The Richter scale measures the size of an earthquake and goes from 1 (small) to 10 (deadly). The largest earthquake ever recorded was a 9.5 in Chile, in 1960. An earthquake measuring 12 would break the Earth in half!

If you are trapped in an avalanche, you have a 93 % chance of survival if you are rescued within 15 minutes. These odds fall to between 20 and 30 % if you are under the snow for 45 minutes. It's very rare for someone to survive longer than two hours.

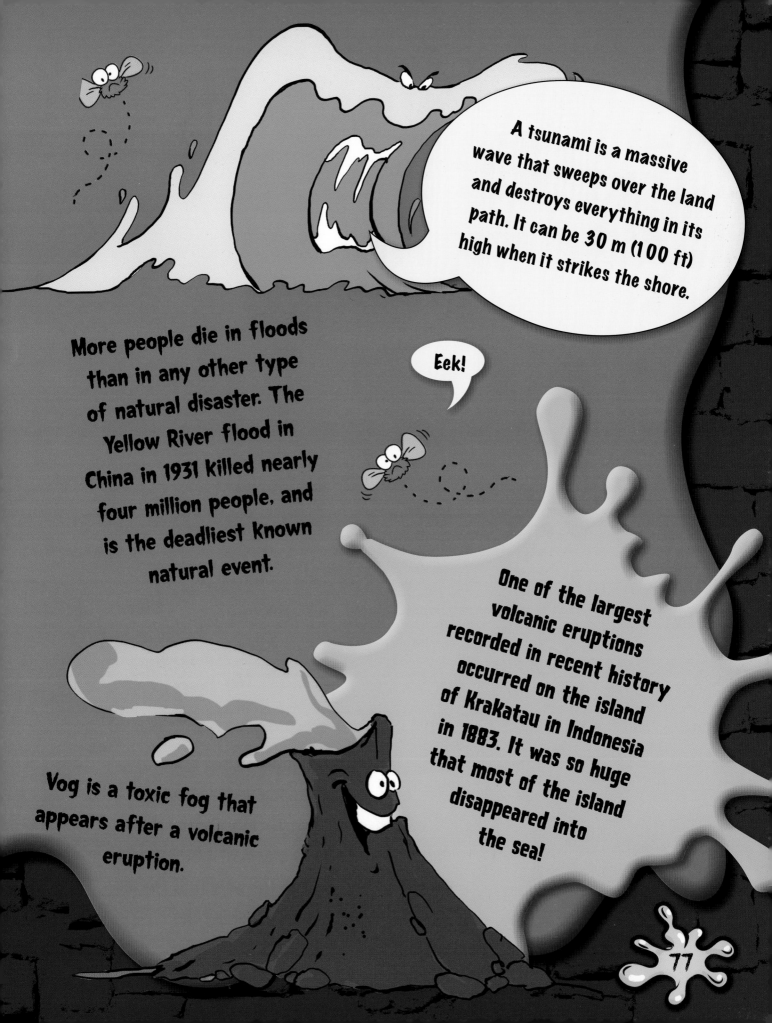

A tsunami is a massive wave that sweeps over the land and destroys everything in its path. It can be 30 m (100 ft) high when it strikes the shore.

More people die in floods than in any other type of natural disaster. The Yellow River flood in China in 1931 killed nearly four million people, and is the deadliest known natural event.

Eek!

One of the largest volcanic eruptions recorded in recent history occurred on the island of Krakatau in Indonesia in 1883. It was so huge that most of the island disappeared into the sea!

Vog is a toxic fog that appears after a volcanic eruption.

77

WILD WEATHER

In 1849 a block of ice that was 6 m (20 ft) long fell from the sky in Scotland. That's one giant hailstone!

If sand is hit by lightning, it can turn to glass!

At any one time, around 100 lightning bolts are striking the Earth.

If ground temperatures are cold enough during a storm, rain can turn to ice as it falls. During the North American ice storm of 1998, many barns collapsed from the weight of the ice on their roofs, crushing the animals inside.

MEDICAL MARVELS

An American called Tom Thompson holds the world record for having the largest metal plate ever inserted into a human skull. Made of titanium, the plate measures 15 x 11 cm (5.9 x 4.33 in).

Doctors have been used as torturers throughout history. They know exactly where it hurts!

Doctors in the old days used leeches to remove people's blood. Today, doctors still use leeches in some surgical procedures, as they produce chemicals that kill pain and keep blood flowing without clotting.

Early anatomists were not allowed to study dead bodies, so they paid grave robbers to steal them. Often, the bodies of executed criminals were stolen and sold.

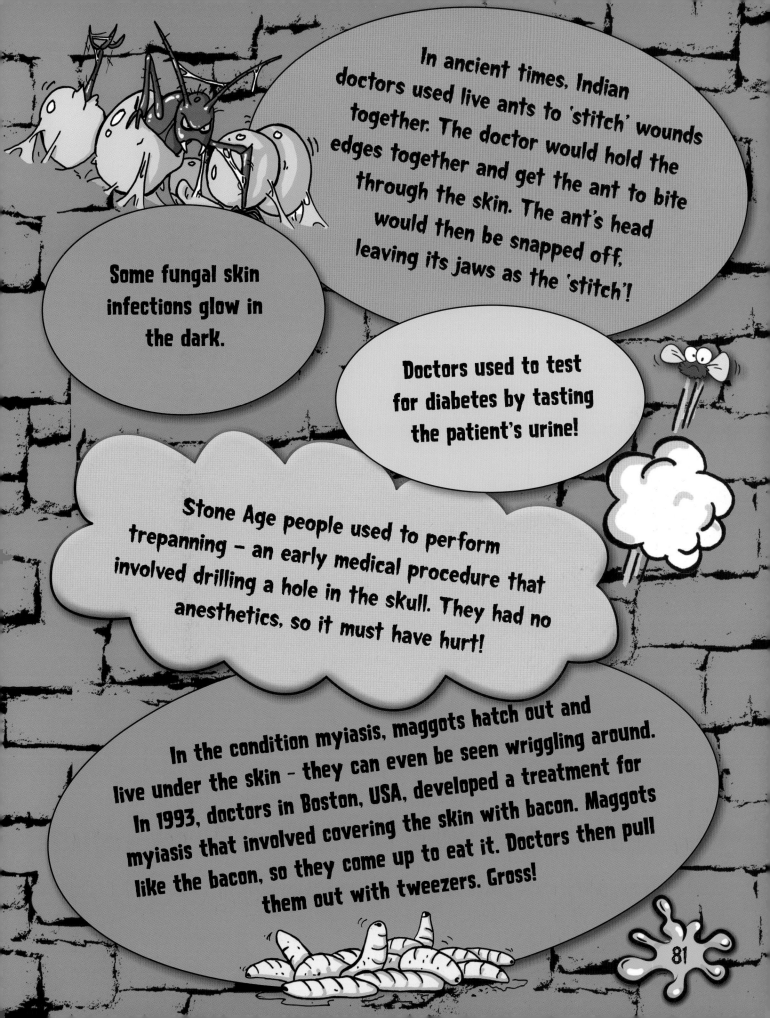

In ancient times, Indian doctors used live ants to 'stitch' wounds together. The doctor would hold the edges together and get the ant to bite through the skin. The ant's head would then be snapped off, leaving its jaws as the 'stitch'!

Some fungal skin infections glow in the dark.

Doctors used to test for diabetes by tasting the patient's urine!

Stone Age people used to perform trepanning – an early medical procedure that involved drilling a hole in the skull. They had no anesthetics, so it must have hurt!

In the condition myiasis, maggots hatch out and live under the skin – they can even be seen wriggling around. In 1993, doctors in Boston, USA, developed a treatment for myiasis that involved covering the skin with bacon. Maggots like the bacon, so they come up to eat it. Doctors then pull them out with tweezers. Gross!

Aconite is one of the most deadly poisons known - yet it is used in homeopathic remedies as a medicine!

Gross!

Deadly hydrogen cyanide gas smells of almonds... but 40 % of people can't smell it.

Arsenic was so commonly used as a poison by murderers in the 1800s, that a law was passed in Britain in 1840 that arsenic must be mixed with a blue or black dye, so that people could see it in their food.

It takes less than 0.1 grams (0.004 ounces) of poison found in parts of the pufferfish to kill an adult human. However, if prepared properly, it can be eaten with no ill effects. How much do you trust the chef...?

Cyanide is a poison that can be made from several plants. A tiny amount is deadly in just five minutes.

Antifreeze is deadly poisonous – some governments insist that manufacturers add a chemical to make it taste horrible to stop people and animals drinking it.

Yuk!

Strychnine poisoning causes extreme muscle spasms. They can be so severe that the body can jerk backward until the heels touch the back of the head and the face is drawn into a terrifying, wide, fixed grin.

The taste of rat poison varies in different countries. It is adapted to suit the food that rats are most used to.

LOOKING PRETTY!

The most bizarre cosmetic procedure has to be tongue-splitting. A scalpel or laser is used to cut down the middle of the tongue and give it a forked appearance. Freaky!

Ambergris is a chemical found in some perfumes, but it originally comes from whale vomit!

Some toiletries and makeup products contain carmine, which is made from crushed beetles!

Body modification fan Erl Van Aken has a flap of skin on his stomach formed into a kind of handle shape that he can put his finger through. Why? Just because!

JewelEye is a body modification procedure available from Dutch eye clinics. The eye membrane is sliced open and a decorative platinum shape is inserted. It's not available anywhere else in the world, as it's dangerous... and just crazy!

Australian performance artist Stelarc had a human ear grafted on to his forearm in the name of art. He can literally turn a deaf ear to anyone who annoys him!

Some cultures have a tradition of earlobe stretching. People wear heavy earrings that can weigh up to 500 g (1 lb) and hang them from huge holes in their earlobes.

Japanese scientists have discovered a way of extracting a vanilla-like fragrance from manure that could be used in cosmetics. Get ready for cow dung bubble bath!

TECHNOLOGY GOES NUTS

It is possible to create fuel from animal fat. It has also been attempted with fat from humans!

Scientists have tried running cars on chicken poop!

A robotic caterpillar controlled by wires can be inserted through a small hole in the chest, and crawl over a person's heart to inject drugs or install implants to repair any damage.

A dentist from New York invented the electric chair.

There are more than 20,000 car crashes involving kangaroos in Australia every year, so a robotic kangaroo-like crash test dummy called Robo-Roo is used to test how badly cars will be damaged.

Chemical engineers have developed a spray-on skin. The special goo is designed to cover soldiers' wounds in war zones and can last for up to two weeks in mud and other nasty germ-filled environments.

Faulty electrical wiring smells like rotten fish!

Hunters in the Amazon heat poison arrow frogs over a fire to sweat the poison out of them. They use the poison to tip their hunting arrows.

Robotarium X in Portugal is the first zoo full of robots, where 45 robots share a steel and glass cage. Some are nice and respond to visitors. Others are nasty and try to bite the tails off their companions. How bizarre!

87

SHOCKING SPACE

Astronauts wear special absorbant underpants during take off, landing and on space walks, as they can't go to the bathroom at these times!

Gross!

The effects of zero gravity on the human body are so severe that astronauts who stay in space for a long time suffer muscle wasting and loss of bone density. They can be unwell for months or sometimes years after their return to Earth.

If you fell into a black hole, your body would be 'spaghettified' – drawn out into an incredibly long, thin strand. Better not try!

When you eventually came out of the black hole, you would be light and ash.

Equipment retrived from the Moon in the 1970s contained germs left there in 1967 – they were still alive!

The 'Vomit Comet' is the name given to an aircraft that flies in such a way that it produces weightlessness. It's used to train astronauts, carry out research and even make movies. It tends to make people sick, as you could probably guess...

Solid waste from space toilets on shuttles is compressed and stored for return to Earth; liquid waste is thrown out into space.

Yuk!

CRAZY SCIENTISTS

A 'body farm' is a research lab where dead bodies are left to decay in various situations. Scientists study their decomposition and the information is used to help police with murder investigations.

A scatologist is a person who studies poop for a living.

Scientists are experimenting with a pill to help people lose weight. The pill swells up to 1,000 times its original size, making the person feel full up, so that they don't eat.

British scientists found that a robotic nose is better at detecting smells if it is given a coating of artificial snot!

Two American scientists have made a computer mouse that is fitted inside the skin of a real, dead mouse. Gross!

Spanish scientist Jose Manuel Rodriguez Delgado invented a radio device called a stimoceiver which could perform a limited sort of mind control!

German doctor, Gunther von Hagens replaces body fluids with plastic to preserve dead bodies and human organs. The corpses are then shown in art exhibitions and used to train doctors.

During World War II, American scientists planned to release bomb-carrying bats over Japan.

Albert Einstein's brain was removed, sliced up and preserved afer his death. It is now kept at McMaster University, Ontario, USA.

INVENTIONS AND DISCOVERIES

In 2006, a crowd control device was patented that shoots a stream of slime at troublemakers so that they slip and fall over, finding it impossible to get up again.

American inventor William Bullock helped to revolutionize the printing industry with his web rotary printing press, developed in 1863. In a bizarre accident, Bullock was killed when he became caught up in one of his machines.

Joseph Gayetty produced the first factory-made toilet paper in New York in 1857 - he was so pleased with his product that he had his name printed on every sheet!

It's an urban myth that Thomas Crapper (1836-1910) invented the flushing toilet! He was simply a successful London plumber with his own brand of toilets.

92

Fritz von Opel, a German car builder, became the first person to fly by rocket power in 1929. He stayed in the air for 75 seconds!

Nasa has developed ways to collect sweat from exercising astronauts to convert into drinking water for them in space. They can also do this with urine!

The yo-yo was invented in the Philippines centuries ago – possibly for use as a weapon! Its history as a children's toy began in 1928 when Pedro Flores opened a factory making them in California.

Eight-year-old Christopher James Wolfe discovered Zuniceratops in 1996 in New Mexico, USA. Just shows that you're never too young to start dinosaur hunting!

DID YOU KNOW?

- Putrescine is a smelly chemical produced by rotting dead bodies, but it is also responsible for bad breath.

- The shiny coating on jellybeans is made from shellac, an excretion from a beetle!

- Dogs will quite happily eat their own vomit.

- The average bath sponge has more bacteria on it than a toilet bowl.

- If you drink too much water, you can make your brain swell up. In severe cases, it stops functioning.

- In the seventeenth century, spiders rolled in butter were recommended as a cure for malaria.

- Germs can pass through ten layers of toilet paper.

- The scientific name for fear of slime is blennophobia.

- Butyric acid is what causes the acrid smell of rancid butter, Parmesan cheese and vomit.

- Pigs will eat any kind of poop – their own, other animals' and even humans'!

- The superbug MRSA can affect healthy people and kills them within four days.

- If a chicken is caught up in a tornado, its feathers can be ripped out, but it can still survive.

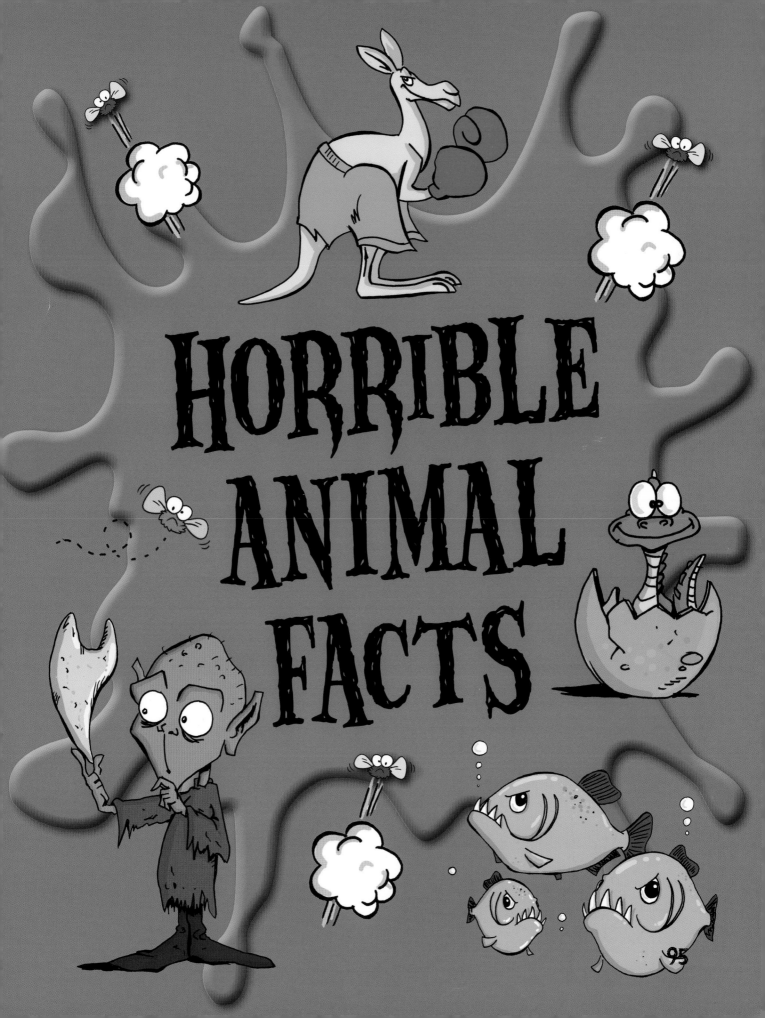

HORRIBLE ANIMAL FACTS

A fully grown python is able to swallow a large pig - whole.

The venom of recluse spiders is necrotic, which means it can dissolve flesh.

The giant cricket of Africa enjoys eating human hair!

Just one gram (0.04 oz) of king cobra venom can kill 150 people.

Each year, rodents cause one billion dollars of damage in the USA alone.

PEE & POOP

The potato beetle larva protects itself from birds that want to eat it by covering itself in its own poisonous poop.

Hippos shower their territory with dung by flapping their tails as they poop.

Baby cockroaches feed on their parents' poop to get the bacteria they need to help them digest plants and vegetables.

The turkey vulture poops onto its own legs to keep them cool.

STINKY BEASTS

Skunks can accurately spray their smelly scent as far as 3 m (10 ft).

Gross!

Cockroaches break wind every fifteen minutes.

Bracken Cave in Texas, USA, is home to 20 million bats. The floor is caked in a thick layer of bat poop that the locals collect to use as fertilizer.

The African zorilla (a type of polecat) could be the smelliest creature on the planet. The stench secreted from its anal glands can be detected up to 1 km (half a mile) away.

Cows release 50 million tonnes of methane gas every year.

Bored monkeys have been known to throw their poop at anyone who happens to be passing... just for fun!

A decomposing sperm whale exploded in Taiwan in 2004 as it was being transported for a post mortem. Nearby buildings and cars were showered with blood, guts and blubber. A build-up of natural gases inside the whale was to blame.

Yuk!

The fart of a female southern pine beetle contains a pheromone called frontalin, which attracts male beetles.

DREADFUL DINOSAURS

The gigantic dinosaur Sauroposeidon could stretch its neck out 17 m (55 ft). That's the same height as eight buses stacked on top of each other!

The insects in the time of the dinosaurs were huge! There were 9 foot long millipede-like creatures, giant flies and massive wasps.

The word dinosaur means 'terrible lizard'.

Scientists use dentists' drills to clean dinosaur bones.

Scientists know what the dinosaurs ate because they study coprolite - that's right, giant fossilized dino poop!

T. rex's teeth were four times longer than a modern tiger's.

Unlike in the movies, Velociraptor did not kill its prey with its razor-sharp claws. It used them to hang on to its prey while attacking it with its teeth, a bit like lions do today.

Cells discovered in a T. rex bone have DNA that so closely resembles that of a bird, that some scientists believe T. rex would have tasted like chicken!

VILE VOMITERS

Birds feed their babies by eating food for them! They go out, eat, then fly back to the nest and vomit up the meal into the babies' mouths. Yummy!

If a predator gets too close to a vulture, it will protect itself by trying to vomit in the predator's eyes, causing a burning sensation.

When a frog is sick, it vomits up its own stomach, which hangs out of its mouth for a short time before it swallows it back down.

Owls swallow their prey (mostly mice and voles) whole. The parts they cannot digest, like fur and bones, are formed into small pellets which the owl throws up.

Vampire bats are surprisingly thoughtful. If a bat is too sick to go out and feed, another bat will suck blood all night, come home, and vomit it up over the unwell bat so that it doesn't miss out on a meal. How kind!

Rats are unable to burp or vomit.

The southern giant petrel bird likes to vomit smelly stomach oils and regurgitated food at predators or nosy humans.

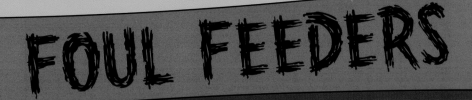

FOUL FEEDERS

A shark can sense even a small amount of blood in water over half a mile (1 km) away.

An octopus has to turn itself inside out to eat, because its mouth is hidden in between its tentacles.

Gross!

A mosquito can drink one and a half times its own weight in blood in a single meal.

The face fly feeds on the mucus produced in a cow's eyes and nostrils.

A leech will only finish sucking blood when it is five times its original size.

There is a type of cockroach in Brazil that likes to eat eyelashes!

Head lice suck blood for about 45 seconds every 2-3 hours, but they can go without a meal for up to two days if they are between heads – on a comb, towel or pillow.

Yuk!

If a rat didn't keep chewing, its lower teeth would eventually grow through its top jaw and up into the roof of its mouth.

ANIMAL ATTACK

The bulldog ant from Australia will sting again and again while holding on with its fierce jaws. It can kill a human in 15 minutes.

Some spiders spit special sticky goo at their prey so that it's literally glued to the spot.

Crocodiles can't bite and chew. Instead, they hold their prey under water until it drowns, then twist their bodies around to tear chunks off the victim.

The tentacles of the deadly box jellyfish contain tiny harpoons which inject poison into its unlucky victim.

Electric eels can deliver a shock of 500 volts to stun their prey into submission.

Scorpions paralyze their prey before they suck the juices out. It's not dead, but it can't escape.

The slime eel, or hagfish, produces slimy mucus from pores in its body if it is disturbed. It throws out strings of mucus which makes the sea around it sticky, gunky and impossible to swim through. They can suffocate on their own slime if they overdo it.

The horned lizard from South America shoots blood out of its eyes when it is attacked.

FEATHERED FREAKS

Penguin urine accounts for nearly 3 % of the ice in Antarctic glaciers.

The burrowing owl of North and South America makes its nest underground, and lines it with cow dung for warmth.

Some birds swallow stones or grit to help break up the food in their stomachs. They then regurgitate them later.

Birds that lay their eggs in the nests of other birds often check to see if their eggs are being cared for. If their eggs have been removed, the birds vandalize the nest, killing any other eggs or chicks.

Woodpeckers slam their heads into trees at a rate of 20 pecks per second. A spongy area behind their beaks acts as a shock absorber and stops them from getting a headache.

The skin and feathers of the pitohui bird are poisonous. Touching them will cause numbness and tingling.

On January 15, 2009, a US Airways plane crash-landed on the Hudson River in New York. A bird had been sucked into one of its engines, causing power failure. Amazingly, no one was harmed!

The lappet-faced vulture of Saudi Arabia is able to strip a small antelope carcass to the bone within 20 minutes.

CREEPY CRAWLIES

Instead of giving birth, a pregnant scorpion sometimes reabsorbs its babies back into its body.

Gross!

If two flies were left to reproduce for a year, without threat from predators, the resulting mass of flies would be the size of planet Earth!

Insect flatulence may account for 20 % of all methane emissions on the planet!

Some types of botfly lay their eggs on the abdomens of fleas or ticks. When they hatch, the baby botflies burrow into the skin of the host and suck the poor victim dry as their first meal.

Because maggots have no teeth, they ooze saliva from of their mouths to liquidize their food before sucking it up.

A cockroach can survive being frozen in a block of ice for two days.

Yuk!

Flea larvae like to eat their parents' poop... or each other!

Only female mosquitos drink human blood. They do it to get the protein they need to lay eggs, which then hatch into more mosquitoes...

MONTSROUS MAMMALS

When an opossum is threatened, it plays dead. It lies still, its tongue hanging out, excretes poop on itself and oozes green slime that smells of rotting flesh.

Rats that hibernate together sometimes get their tails tied up in a knot. If they urinate over themselves in the winter, they can freeze together in a block. A knot of rats is called a king rat.

Being trampled by a cow is the cause of death for around 100 people each year.

In Tasmania, kangaroo manure has been used to make environmentally friendly paper.

The naked mole rat is the ugliest mammal in the world. It looks like a wrinkly sausage with very short legs and huge, protruding teeth. It has no hair anywhere except on the inside of its mouth.

Hippos kill more people per year than any other mammal in Africa! They like to overturn boats, trample people and even use their massive mouths to bite people's heads off.

Sneaky polar bears wait by holes in the ice and eat seals when they come up for air!

FREAKY FISH

A shark will eat parts of its own body that have been cut off or bitten off by another animal.

The deep-sea gulper eel can eat fish larger than itself. It can open its mouth so wide that its jaw bends back on itself at an angle of more than 180 degrees.

When a fish called the Pacific grenadier is pulled out of the sea by fishermen, the change in pressure makes gas inside it expand quickly and its stomach pops out of its mouth.

The teeth of a viperfish are half the length of its head, so it can't close its mouth! It has to open its jaws very wide in order to swallow.

Some of the items found inside sharks' stomachs include a horse's head, a porcupine, parts of bicycles and cars, a sheep, a chicken coop – and even a metal suit with the remains of a French soldier inside!

The anglerfish has a glowing blob attached to a spike at the front of its head. In the deep, dark sea the glowing blob attracts small prey, which the anglerfish then sucks in and gobbles up.

Sharks don't have a urinary tract so their urine leaks out of their skin.

Piranhas' teeth are so strong that they can bite neatly through a steel fishing hook.

BADLY BEHAVED

Slugs like drinking beer! Some gardeners leave traps for them, so that the slugs get drunk and drown.

Gross!

The robber crab got its nickname from its habit of stealing shiny things like pots and pans from people's houses!

Termites fart out between 20 million and 80 million tons of gas every year (not each, all together).

Cockroaches will eat each other when there's not much food around. After ripping open their victim's stomach, they tear out their insides.

The female black widow spider eats the male after mating, sometimes eating up to 25 partners a day. Now that's a real man-eater!

A vampire finch in the Galápagos Islands pecks holes in other birds to feed on their blood.

Yuk!

You could get bitten by a crocodile, but alligators don't like the taste of people.

Leeches don't just suck from the outside of your body. If you drink water with a leech in, it can attach to the inside of your mouth or throat. If you swim in a river, leeches can go into your bottom and suck you from the inside.

WILD 'N' WET

Leatherback turtles have spines in their throats! These stop the jellyfish they eat from sliding back out of their mouths.

If you're bitten by a moray eel, the only way to get it off is to kill it, cut the head off and break the jaws. It won't let go while it's alive.

A female tiger shark carries several babies during pregnancy but only gives birth to one. In the womb, the strongest baby eats the others until it is the only one left.

If you kept a goldfish in a darkened room for long enough, it would eventually turn white.

Even after it has been cut off, an octopus tentacle will carry on wriggling for some time.

Most tropical marine fish could survive in a tank filled with human blood because of all the oxygen it contains.

The parrotfish makes itself a kind of mucus sleeping bag. This masks its smell from predators and helps keep parasites away.

The jaws of the snapping turtle are so powerful that they can rip off a human finger!

PREPOSTEROUS PETS

Every dog's anal scent glands give off a unique smell. Dogs put their tails between their legs to cover up the scent.

Pet food manufacturers once developed a cat food that tasted like mice, but the cats didn't like it!

During heavy downpours in 17th-century England, many of the stray cats and dogs would drown and float down the narrow streets. It is said this is where the expression 'raining cats and dogs' comes from.

The punishment for killing a greyhound in ancient Egypt was the same as for killing a man.

The largest number of mice caught by a single cat is 28,899 over a 21-year period. That's about four mice a day, every day!

Rudi the German Giant rabbit from Berlin, Germany, is thought to be the world's largest pet rabbit, tipping the scales at a whopping 10 kg (22 lb). Despite her 94 cm (3 ft 1 in) length, Rudi is still growing.

Dachshund dogs were originally bred for killing badgers, rabbits and foxes.

Rabbits partially digest the grass they eat and then excrete it as soft, gluey pellets. They then eat these pellets to finish digesting their meal properly. Yummy!

THAT'S GROSS

A jellyfish excretes poop through its mouth – it has only one opening and uses it for all purposes.

A starving mouse will eat its own tail.

Rats have been known to transmit several potentially fatal diseases to humans, including plague, Weil's disease and Q fever.

The contents of a sloth's stomach can take up to a month to be digested completely. That's a lot of rotten twigs and berries...

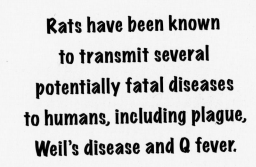

A head louse can lay 200–300 eggs during its life of around 30 days. The eggs only take five to ten days to hatch and start feeding.

The pearl fish swims into a sea cucumber's bottom and lives inside it during the day, coming out at night. The sea cucumber breathes through its anus, so it can't keep the fish out!

Yuk!

Mosquitoes love stinky human feet because of the enzymes found on them.

Light spots on surfaces of food show that a fly has vomited something up and tasted the surface. Dark spots are fly poop.

CRAZY CRITTERS

Crocodiles' jaws are very weak when opening. They can be held shut with nothing more than an elastic band.

The burrowing owl makes its nest underground and lines it with cow dung.

Bird droppings can take on the hue of certain foods that haven't been completely digested. Purple pigeon droppings are particularly common in the UK due to the berries they eat.

The bite of a Komodo dragon isn't poisonous, but there are so many bacteria in their mouths – growing in rotten meat between their teeth – that a bite from one often leads to blood poisoning and death.

In 1939, a student at Harvard University, USA, was dared to swallow a live goldfish for a bet. He did, and goldfish swallowing became a university craze.

Fearsome driver ants move in such massive colonies that they can strip the flesh from any animal they come across down to the bone. They have been known to completely devour wounded lions and crocodiles.

Pigs do not sweat so they roll about in mud to keep cool in hot weather.

Elephants have been known to stay standing up long after they have died!

127